M000309594

mary and Joseph

(Help of Christians-
Holy Hill, Wisconsin)

Models of Faith and Love

First century

Feast of the Holy Family:

Sunday after Christmas
(or December 30 if Sunday after
Christmas is January 1)

Patronage:

Christian families

Text by Barbara Yoffie
Illustrated by Katherine A. Borgatti

Liguori

Dedication

**To my family:
my parents Jim and Peg,
my husband Bill,
our son Sam and daughter-in-law Erin,
and our precious grandchildren
Ben, Lucas, and Andrew**

**To all the children I have had the privilege of
teaching throughout the years.**

Imprimi Potest:
Harry Grile, CSsR, Provincial
Denver Province, The Redemptorists

Published by Liguori Publications
Liguori, Missouri 63057

To order, call 800-325-9521
www.liguori.org

Copyright © 2013 Liguori Publications

All rights reserved. No part of this publication may be reproduced, stored in
a retrieval system, or transmitted in any form or by any means—electronic,
mechanical, photocopy, recording, or any other—except for brief quotations in
printed reviews, without the prior written permission of Liguori Publications.

p ISBN: 978-0-7648-2335-0
e ISBN: 978-0-7648-6845-0

Liguori Publications, a nonprofit corporation, is an apostolate of The
Redemptorists. To learn more about The Redemptorists, visit Redemptorists.com.

Printed in the United States of America
16 15 14 13 / 5 4 3 2
First Edition

Dear Parents and Teachers:

Saints and Me! is a series of children's books about saints, with six books in each set. The first set is titled *Saints of North America.* This second set, *Saints of Christmas,* selects seven heavenly heroes who teach us to love the Infant Jesus. Some saints in this set have feast days within Advent and Christmas time, but others are celebrated within ordinary time and Easter time. We selected these saints based on their connection to the Christmas story and how they inspire us to let the mystery of Christ's birth grow within our hearts.

Saints of Christmas includes the heroic lives of seven saints from different times and places who loved Jesus. Saints Mary and Joseph witnessed the miracle of God's abundant love for humanity as our Infant Savior entered the world to bring us home to God. Saint Lucy followed Jesus in a time when Christianity was against the law. The story of Saint Nicholas was so incredible that it inspired our secular notion of Santa Claus. Saint Francis of Assisi added much flavor to our current Christmas traditions. Saint Martin de Porres is a biracial saint who teaches us about divine love for all people. And a saint of our own era, Gianna Beretta Molla, witnessed a deep belief in the gift of life.

Which saint cared for slaves from Africa? Who became a doctor and mother? What saints were present at Jesus' birth in Bethlehem? Who desired to be a knight? Which saint was a bishop of a seaport city? Do you know which saint's name means "light?" Find the answers in the *Saints of Christmas* set, part of the *Saints and Me!* series, and help your child identify with the lives of the saints.

Introduce your children or students to the *Saints and Me!* series as they:

—**READ** about the lives of the saints and are inspired by their stories.

—**PRAY** to the saints for their intercession.

—**CELEBRATE** the saints and relate to their lives.

saints of christmas

advent	**week 1**		
	week 2		
	week 3		
	week 4		
christmas	**week 5**		
	week 6		

 Mary and Joseph   Francis of Assisi

Lucy   Martin de Porres

 Nicholas of Myra   Gianna Beretta Molla

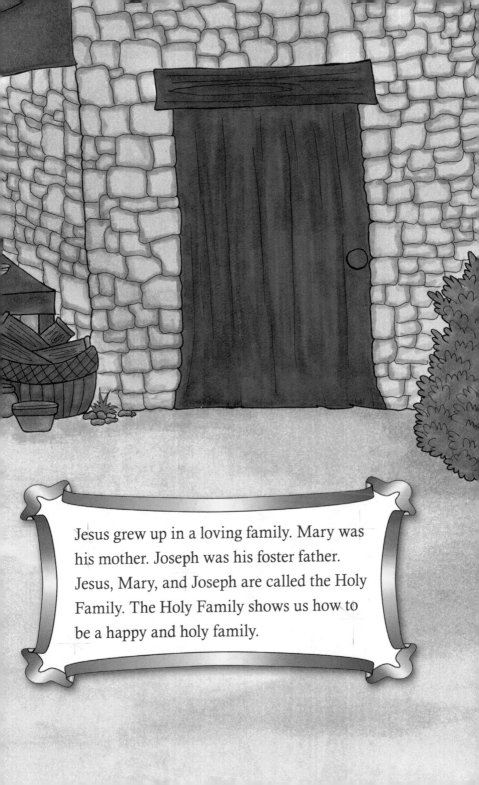

Jesus grew up in a loving family. Mary was his mother. Joseph was his foster father. Jesus, Mary, and Joseph are called the Holy Family. The Holy Family shows us how to be a happy and holy family.

Mary grew up in the town of Nazareth. Her parents, Anne and Joachim, loved Mary very much. They taught her about God. Mary prayed every day. She loved God with all her heart.

Joseph was a kind and gentle man. He lived in Nazareth, too. Joseph was a carpenter. He worked all day in his shop making tools and wooden furniture. Joseph loved Mary, and they were going to be married.

One day, an angel appeared to Mary and said, "God loves you, Mary. He wants you to be the mother of his Son." But Mary did not understand the angel's message. "You will have a baby boy, and his name will be Jesus. It is God's plan," said the angel. Mary replied, "I will do what God asks of me."

An angel appeared to Joseph in a dream. The angel told Joseph that Mary's baby was God's Son. Joseph began to understand the wonderful message from God. Soon Mary and Joseph were married. They were very happy.

A short time before Jesus was born, Mary and Joseph went to Bethlehem. When they got to the city it was busy and crowded with people. They had no place to stay, and Mary was very tired. "Do not worry Mary, I will take care of you," Joseph promised.

He found a small cave near a stable. They would be safe here and Mary could rest. Later that night, Jesus, the Son of God was born. "He is a beautiful and special baby," Joseph whispered to Mary. Mary and Joseph were filled with joy.

Shepherds in a nearby field saw an angel.
"A child is born in Bethlehem. He is God's
Son," the angel told them. Then many
angels filled the dark sky. "Glory to God.
Peace on earth," they sang.

The shepherds ran as fast as they could to Bethlehem. They found Mary, Joseph, and the Baby Jesus. He was sleeping in a manger, wrapped in cloth. "This is God's Son," a shepherd cried out.

Later, three wise men, or Magi, came to see the Baby Jesus. They followed a bright star in the sky. The Magi brought special gifts for the baby because they knew he was the Son of God.

A few months passed, and Mary and Joseph took Jesus to the Temple. Here they met a man named Simeon and a woman named Anna. Simeon held Jesus in his arms and smiled. Anna smiled, too.

The Holy Family returned to Nazareth.
Jesus' parents taught him many things.
They taught him how to pray. They told
him stories about their faith. Joseph showed
Jesus how to make things out of wood.

When Jesus was twelve, he went to Jerusalem for the feast of Passover with his family. Many people were in the Temple praying. Mary and Joseph left, but Jesus stayed in the Temple. Later, they looked for Jesus and could not find him.

Mary and Joseph hurried back to the Temple.
Jesus was talking to the teachers. "We were
so worried about you," Mary told Jesus.
"I am here in my Father's house," he said.
"Come, let us go home now," said Joseph.

Jesus, Mary, and Joseph spent many more happy years in Nazareth. After Joseph died, Jesus took care of Mary until it was time for him to leave home. Then, Jesus went to towns and villages to teach people about God.

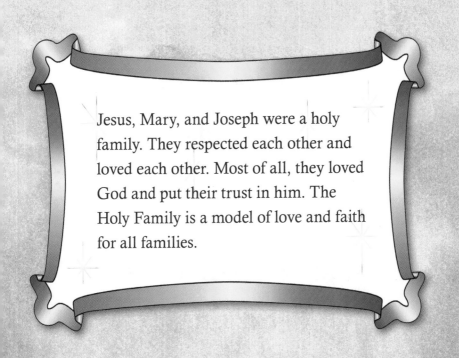

Jesus, Mary, and Joseph were a holy family. They respected each other and loved each other. Most of all, they loved God and put their trust in him. The Holy Family is a model of love and faith for all families.

A family loves and a family shares.
But most of all a family cares.

Dear God.

I love you.

Mary, Joseph, and Jesus

loved you

and trusted in your

goodness.

Bless my family

with your love.

Protect us and fill us

with peace.

Amen.

NEW WORDS (Glossary)

Angel: A spiritual being; God's helper and messenger

Carpenter: A person who works with and makes things out of wood

Foster father: A man who raises a child as his own in place of the real father

Magi: The wise men who came to see Baby Jesus in Bethlehem

Manger: A feeding box for farm animals

Passover: A Jewish feast that celebrates the Hebrews leaving Egypt

Stable: A building where animals are fed and kept safe

Temple: A place of worship and learning for the Jewish people

Liguori Publications
saints and me! series

SAINTS OF CHRISTMAS

Collect the entire set!

LUCY

A Light for Jesus

Francis of Assisi

Keeper of Creation

martin de porres

A Beggar for Justice

nicholas of myra

Giver of Many Gifts

Gianna Beretta molla

Wife, Mother, and Doctor

mary and Joseph

Models of Faith and Love

**SAINTS OF CHRISTMAS
ACTIVITY BOOK**

Reproducible activities
for all 6 saints in the series